PURE OCD WORKBOOK

PRACTICAL WORKSHEETS FOR TAMING INTRUSIVE THOUGHTS

Copyright 2023 © MESLOUB IHEB

PURE OCD SYMPTOMS

PURE "O" SYMPTOMS	SEVERITY	MON	TUES	WED	THUR	FRI	SAT	SUN

PURE O
CBT WORKSHEET

Write down your thoughts, feelings, and behaviors related to your Pure O symptoms. Record the date, time, and any triggers that led to your symptoms.

- ⊘ —— : ——
- ⊘ —— : ——
- ⊘ —— : ——
- ⊘ —— : ——
- ⊘ —— : ——
- ⊘ —— : ——

Daily Mood Checker ✓

ANGRY	☐
ANNOYED	☐
ANXIOUS	☐
ASHAMED	☐
AWKWARD	☐
BRAVE	☐
CALM	☐
CHEERFUL	☐
CHILL	☐
CONFUSED	☐
DISCOURAGED	☐
DISTRACTED	☐
EMBARRASSED	☐
EXCITED	☐
FRIENDLY	☐
GUILTY	☐
HAPPY	☐
HOPEFUL	☐
LONELY	☐
LOVED	☐
NERVOUS	☐
OFFENDED	☐
SCARED	☐
THOUGHTFUL	☐
TIRED	☐
UNCOMFORTABLE	☐
UNSURE	☐

PURE OCD
ERP WORKSHEET

01 - IDENTIFY TRIGGERS: IDENTIFY THE SPECIFIC TRIGGERS THAT CAUSE YOUR INTRUSIVE THOUGHTS.
(A CERTAIN IDEA OR FEELING)
(A SPECIFIC SITUATION OR THING).

02 - ONCE YOU'VE IDENTIFIED YOUR TRIGGERS, CREATE A HIERARCHY OF EXPOSURE TASKS, START WITH THE TASK OF LEAST ANXIETY AND EXPOSE YOURSELF TO THE TRIGGER FOR A SET AMOUNT OF TIME WITHOUT ENGAGING IN ANY MENTAL COMPULSIVE BEHAVIORS. THIS WILL BE DIFFICULT. TRY TO RESIST PERFORMING ANY COMPULSIVE BEHAVIORS AS THIS WILL ONLY REINFORCE THE OBSESSION.

Triggers Checklist ✔

- ANGRY ☐
- ANNOYED ☐
- ANXIOUS ☐
- ASHAMED ☐
- AWKWARD ☐
- BRAVE ☐
- CALM ☐
- CHEERFUL ☐
- CHILL ☐
- CONFUSED ☐
- DISCOURAGED ☐
- DISTRACTED ☐
- EMBARRASSED ☐
- EXCITED ☐
- FRIENDLY ☐
- GUILTY ☐
- HAPPY ☐
- HOPEFUL ☐
- LONELY ☐
- LOVED ☐
- NERVOUS ☐
- OFFENDED ☐
- SCARED ☐
- THOUGHTFUL ☐
- TIRED ☐
- UNCOMFORTABLE ☐
- UNSURE ☐

PURE OCD
ERP WORKSHEET

03- CONTINUE EXPOSING YOURSELF TO THE TRIGGER UNTIL YOUR ANXIETY LEVEL DECREASES. IT IS IMPORTANT TO MAINTAIN EXPOSURE FOR A SUFFICIENT PERIOD OF TIME AS YOUR BRAIN WILL BECOME ACCUSTOMED TO THE ANXIETY AND WILL NATURALLY DECREASE.

Daily Mood Checker ✔

04- ONCE YOU HAVE BECOME ACCUSTOMED TO THE PREVIOUS EXPOSURE TASK, MOVE ON TO THE NEXT TASK THAT YOU HAVE IDENTIFIED IN THE HIERARCHY, GRADUALLY WORKING ON THE TASK OF MOST CONCERN AND CONTINUING EXPOSURE TO IT AT THE SAME LEVEL FOR HABITUATION.

NOTE

ERP therapy can be difficult and may take time to show results. But the most important thing is to train regularly and constantly to make progress....

OVERCOMING PURE O.C.D THROUGH D.B.T

IN THIS TABLE, TRY TO UNDERSTAND THE OUTBURSTS OF INTRUSIVE THOUGHTS THAT YOU EXPERIENCE FROM TIME TO TIME.
(AT WORK, MEETINGS...ETC)
DISCUSS THEIR IMPACT ON ASPECTS OF YOUR LIFE, AND WHAT COPING SKILLS DO YOU THINK WORK WHEN YOU USE THEM? CONSISTENTLY RATE HOW SUCCESSFUL YOU ARE IN APPLYING THESE SKILLS?

• DISTRESS • INTERPERSONAL EFFECTIVENESS • EMOTIONAL REGULATION PROBLEMS	COPING SKILLS OR PREVENTION IDEAS OR SKILLS

DAILY MOOD CYCLE

Instructions: Think about your day from start to finish. Color the first square to express your feelings each time of the day. Next, write a word that reflects your feelings, and draw in the circle a picture of your face that reflects your feelings at that moment.

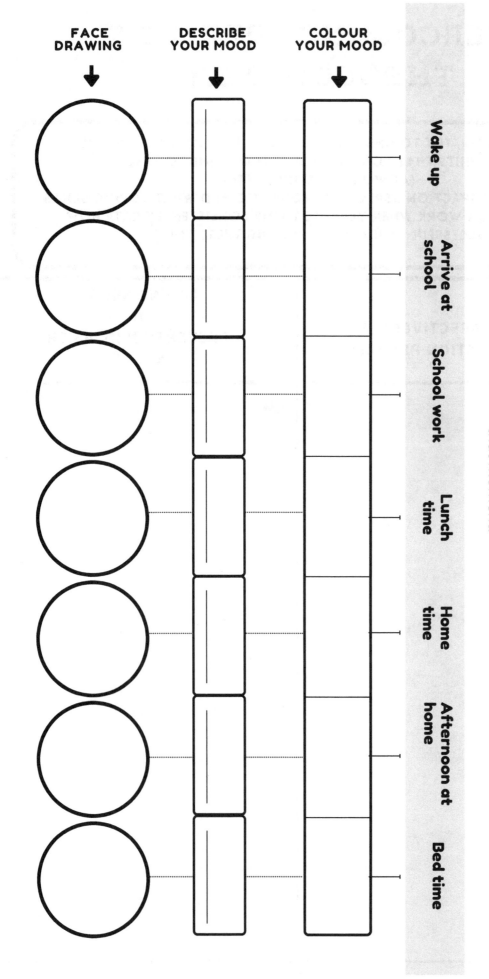

FACE DRAWING

DESCRIBE YOUR MOOD

COLOUR YOUR MOOD

Wake up

Arrive at school

School work

Lunch time

Home time

Afternoon at home

Bed time

CHALLENGING PURE O - DBT WORKSHEET

A NEW DAY AND AN EFFECTIVE PLAN WORKSHEET

Date :..

This section is dedicated to recording all the events of your daily experience with pure obsessive-compulsive disorder and the effects of intrusive thoughts on your quality of life.

_____

_____

_____

_____

_____

_____

_____

_____

_____

_____

_____

_____

_____

_____

_____

_____

PURE OCD SYMPTOMS

PURE "O" SYMPTOMS	SEVERITY	MON	TUES	WED	THUR	FRI	SAT	SUN

Write down your thoughts, feelings, and behaviors related to your Pure O symptoms. Record the date, time, and any triggers that led to your symptoms.

⊘ —:—

⊘ —:—

⊘ —:—

⊘ —:—

⊘ —:—

⊘ —:—

Daily Mood Checker	✓
ANGRY	☐
ANNOYED	☐
ANXIOUS	☐
ASHAMED	☐
AWKWARD	☐
BRAVE	☐
CALM	☐
CHEERFUL	☐
CHILL	☐
CONFUSED	☐
DISCOURAGED	☐
DISTRACTED	☐
EMBARRASSED	☐
EXCITED	☐
FRIENDLY	☐
GUILTY	☐
HAPPY	☐
HOPEFUL	☐
LONELY	☐
LOVED	☐
NERVOUS	☐
OFFENDED	☐
SCARED	☐
THOUGHTFUL	☐
TIRED	☐
UNCOMFORTABLE	☐
UNSURE	☐

PURE OCD
ERP WORKSHEET

Date :

Sleep quality :

01 - IDENTIFY TRIGGERS: IDENTIFY THE SPECIFIC
TRIGGERS THAT CAUSE YOUR INTRUSIVE THOUGHTS.
(A CERTAIN IDEA OR FEELING)
(A SPECIFIC SITUATION OR THING).

02 - ONCE YOU'VE IDENTIFIED YOUR TRIGGERS, CREATE A
HIERARCHY OF EXPOSURE TASKS, START WITH THE TASK
OF LEAST ANXIETY AND EXPOSE YOURSELF TO THE
TRIGGER FOR A SET AMOUNT OF TIME WITHOUT
ENGAGING IN ANY MENTAL COMPULSIVE BEHAVIORS. THIS
WILL BE DIFFICULT. TRY TO RESIST PERFORMING ANY
COMPULSIVE BEHAVIORS AS THIS WILL ONLY REINFORCE
THE OBSESSION.

Triggers Checklist

- [ ] ANGRY
- [ ] ANNOYED
- [ ] ANXIOUS
- [ ] ASHAMED
- [ ] AWKWARD
- [ ] BRAVE
- [ ] CALM
- [ ] CHEERFUL
- [ ] CHILL
- [ ] CONFUSED
- [ ] DISCOURAGED
- [ ] DISTRACTED
- [ ] EMBARRASSED
- [ ] EXCITED
- [ ] FRIENDLY
- [ ] GUILTY
- [ ] HAPPY
- [ ] HOPEFUL
- [ ] LONELY
- [ ] LOVED
- [ ] NERVOUS
- [ ] OFFENDED
- [ ] SCARED
- [ ] THOUGHTFUL
- [ ] TIRED
- [ ] UNCOMFORTABLE
- [ ] UNSURE

PURE OCD
ERP WORKSHEET

03- CONTINUE EXPOSING YOURSELF TO THE TRIGGER UNTIL YOUR ANXIETY LEVEL DECREASES. IT IS IMPORTANT TO MAINTAIN EXPOSURE FOR A SUFFICIENT PERIOD OF TIME AS YOUR BRAIN WILL BECOME ACCUSTOMED TO THE ANXIETY AND WILL NATURALLY DECREASE.

Daily Mood Checker ✓

04- ONCE YOU HAVE BECOME ACCUSTOMED TO THE PREVIOUS EXPOSURE TASK, MOVE ON TO THE NEXT TASK THAT YOU HAVE IDENTIFIED IN THE HIERARCHY, GRADUALLY WORKING ON THE TASK OF MOST CONCERN AND CONTINUING EXPOSURE TO IT AT THE SAME LEVEL FOR HABITUATION.

NOTE

ERP therapy can be difficult and may take time to show results. But the most important thing is to train regularly and constantly to make progress....

OVERCOMING PURE O.C.D THROUGH D.B.T

IN THIS TABLE, TRY TO UNDERSTAND THE OUTBURSTS OF INTRUSIVE THOUGHTS THAT YOU EXPERIENCE FROM TIME TO TIME.
(AT WORK, MEETINGS...ETC)
DISCUSS THEIR IMPACT ON ASPECTS OF YOUR LIFE, AND WHAT COPING SKILLS DO YOU THINK WORK WHEN YOU USE THEM? CONSISTENTLY RATE HOW SUCCESSFUL YOU ARE IN APPLYING THESE SKILLS?

• DISTRESS • INTERPERSONAL EFFECTIVENESS • EMOTIONAL REGULATION PROBLEMS	COPING SKILLS OR PREVENTION IDEAS OR SKILLS

DAILY MOOD CYCLE

Instructions: Think about your day from start to finish. Color the first square to express your feelings each time of the day. Next, write a word that reflects your feelings, and draw in the circle a picture of your face that reflects your feelings at that moment.

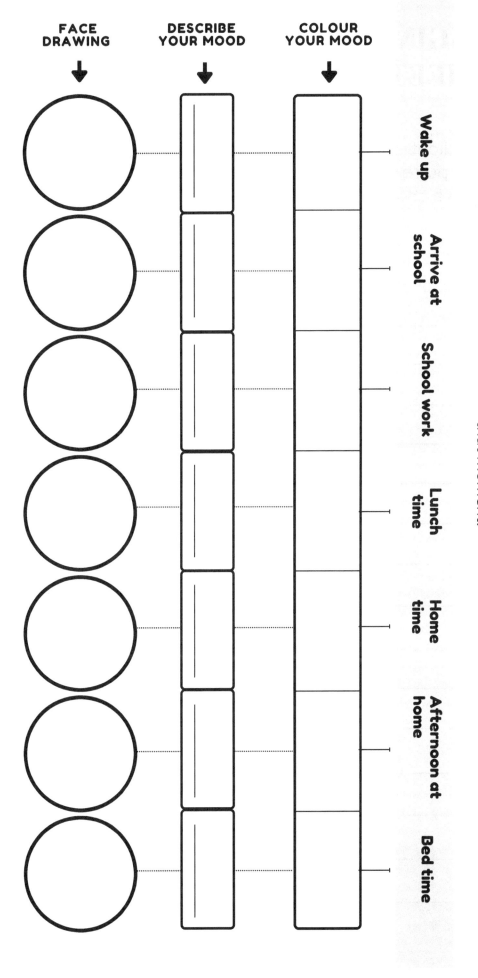

FACE DRAWING

DESCRIBE YOUR MOOD

COLOUR YOUR MOOD

Wake up

Arrive at school

School work

Lunch time

Home time

Afternoon at home

Bed time

CHALLENGING PURE O - DBT WORKSHEET

A NEW DAY AND AN EFFECTIVE PLAN WORKSHEET

Date :....................................

This section is dedicated to recording all the events of your daily experience with pure obsessive-compulsive disorder and the effects of intrusive thoughts on your quality of life.

_____

_____

_____

_____

_____

_____

_____

_____

_____

_____

_____

_____

_____

_____

_____

_____

_____

PURE OCD SYMPTOMS

PURE "O" SYMPTOMS	SEVERITY	MON	TUES	WED	THUR	FRI	SAT	SUN

PURE O
CBT WORKSHEET

Write down your thoughts, feelings, and behaviors related to your Pure O symptoms. Record the date, time, and any triggers that led to your symptoms.

⊘ —:— ....

....

....

....

⊘ —:— ....

....

....

....

⊘ —:— ....

....

....

....

⊘ —:— ....

....

....

....

⊘ —:— ....

....

....

....

⊘ —:— ....

....

Daily Mood Checker ♡

ANGRY	☐
ANNOYED	☐
ANXIOUS	☐
ASHAMED	☐
AWKWARD	☐
BRAVE	☐
CALM	☐
CHEERFUL	☐
CHILL	☐
CONFUSED	☐
DISCOURAGED	☐
DISTRACTED	☐
EMBARRASSED	☐
EXCITED	☐
FRIENDLY	☐
GUILTY	☐
HAPPY	☐
HOPEFUL	☐
LONELY	☐
LOVED	☐
NERVOUS	☐
OFFENDED	☐
SCARED	☐
THOUGHTFUL	☐
TIRED	☐
UNCOMFORTABLE	☐
UNSURE	☐

PURE OCD
ERP WORKSHEET

01 - IDENTIFY TRIGGERS: IDENTIFY THE SPECIFIC TRIGGERS THAT CAUSE YOUR INTRUSIVE THOUGHTS. (A CERTAIN IDEA OR FEELING) (A SPECIFIC SITUATION OR THING).

02 - ONCE YOU'VE IDENTIFIED YOUR TRIGGERS, CREATE A HIERARCHY OF EXPOSURE TASKS, START WITH THE TASK OF LEAST ANXIETY AND EXPOSE YOURSELF TO THE TRIGGER FOR A SET AMOUNT OF TIME WITHOUT ENGAGING IN ANY MENTAL COMPULSIVE BEHAVIORS. THIS WILL BE DIFFICULT. TRY TO RESIST PERFORMING ANY COMPULSIVE BEHAVIORS AS THIS WILL ONLY REINFORCE THE OBSESSION.

Triggers Checklist

- ANGRY ☐
- ANNOYED ☐
- ANXIOUS ☐
- ASHAMED ☐
- AWKWARD ☐
- BRAVE ☐
- CALM ☐
- CHEERFUL ☐
- CHILL ☐
- CONFUSED ☐
- DISCOURAGED ☐
- DISTRACTED ☐
- EMBARRASSED ☐
- EXCITED ☐
- FRIENDLY ☐
- GUILTY ☐
- HAPPY ☐
- HOPEFUL ☐
- LONELY ☐
- LOVED ☐
- NERVOUS ☐
- OFFENDED ☐
- SCARED ☐
- THOUGHTFUL ☐
- TIRED ☐
- UNCOMFORTABLE ☐
- UNSURE ☐

PURE OCD
ERP WORKSHEET

03- CONTINUE EXPOSING YOURSELF TO THE TRIGGER UNTIL YOUR ANXIETY LEVEL DECREASES. IT IS IMPORTANT TO MAINTAIN EXPOSURE FOR A SUFFICIENT PERIOD OF TIME AS YOUR BRAIN WILL BECOME ACCUSTOMED TO THE ANXIETY AND WILL NATURALLY DECREASE.

Daily Mood Checker ✔

04- ONCE YOU HAVE BECOME ACCUSTOMED TO THE PREVIOUS EXPOSURE TASK, MOVE ON TO THE NEXT TASK THAT YOU HAVE IDENTIFIED IN THE HIERARCHY, GRADUALLY WORKING ON THE TASK OF MOST CONCERN AND CONTINUING EXPOSURE TO IT AT THE SAME LEVEL FOR HABITUATION.

NOTE

ERP therapy can be difficult and may take time to show results. But the most important thing is to train regularly and constantly to make progress....

OVERCOMING PURE O.C.D
THROUGH D.B.T

IN THIS TABLE, TRY TO UNDERSTAND THE OUTBURSTS OF INTRUSIVE
THOUGHTS THAT YOU EXPERIENCE FROM TIME TO TIME.
(AT WORK, MEETINGS...ETC)
DISCUSS THEIR IMPACT ON ASPECTS OF YOUR LIFE, AND WHAT COPING SKILLS
DO YOU THINK WORK WHEN YOU USE THEM? CONSISTENTLY RATE HOW
SUCCESSFUL YOU ARE IN APPLYING THESE SKILLS?

• DISTRESS • INTERPERSONAL EFFECTIVENESS • EMOTIONAL REGULATION PROBLEMS	COPING SKILLS OR PREVENTION IDEAS OR SKILLS

DAILY MOOD CYCLE

Instructions: Think about your day from start to finish. Color the first square to express your feelings each time of the day. Next, write a word that reflects your feelings, and draw in the circle a picture of your face that reflects your feelings at that moment.

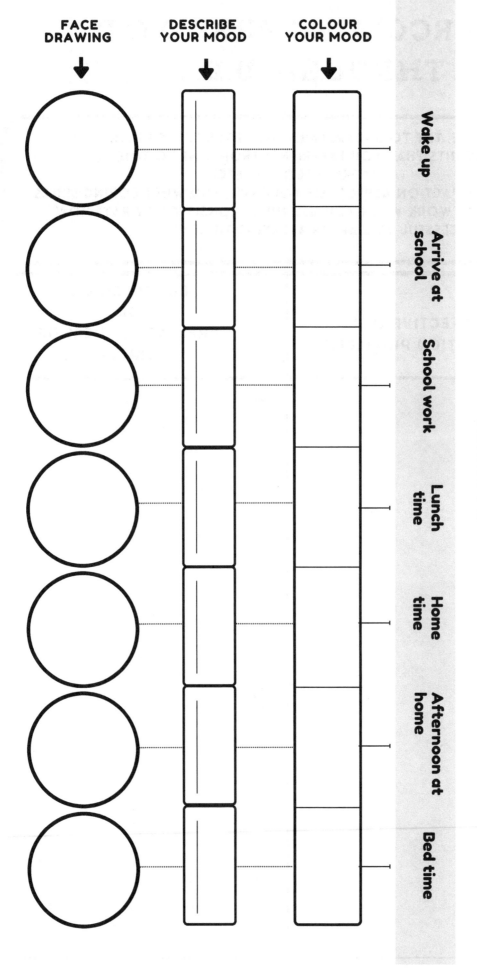

FACE DRAWING

DESCRIBE YOUR MOOD

COLOUR YOUR MOOD

Wake up

Arrive at school

School work

Lunch time

Home time

Afternoon at home

Bed time

CHALLENGING PURE O - DBT WORKSHEET

Date :..

This section is dedicated to recording all the events of your daily experience with pure obsessive-compulsive disorder and the effects of intrusive thoughts on your quality of life.

_____

_____

_____

_____

_____

_____

_____

_____

_____

_____

_____

_____

_____

_____

PURE OCD SYMPTOMS

PURE "O" SYMPTOMS	SEVERITY	MON	TUES	WED	THUR	FRI	SAT	SUN

PURE O
CBT WORKSHEET

Write down your thoughts, feelings, and behaviors related to your Pure O symptoms. Record the date, time, and any triggers that led to your symptoms.

⊘ __ : __

⊘ __ : __

⊘ __ : __

⊘ __ : __

⊘ __ : __

⊘ __ : __

Daily Mood Checker ✔

ANGRY	☐
ANNOYED	☐
ANXIOUS	☐
ASHAMED	☐
AWKWARD	☐
BRAVE	☐
CALM	☐
CHEERFUL	☐
CHILL	☐
CONFUSED	☐
DISCOURAGED	☐
DISTRACTED	☐
EMBARRASSED	☐
EXCITED	☐
FRIENDLY	☐
GUILTY	☐
HAPPY	☐
HOPEFUL	☐
LONELY	☐
LOVED	☐
NERVOUS	☐
OFFENDED	☐
SCARED	☐
THOUGHTFUL	☐
TIRED	☐
UNCOMFORTABLE	☐
UNSURE	☐

PURE OCD
ERP WORKSHEET

01 - IDENTIFY TRIGGERS: IDENTIFY THE SPECIFIC TRIGGERS THAT CAUSE YOUR INTRUSIVE THOUGHTS.
(A CERTAIN IDEA OR FEELING)
(A SPECIFIC SITUATION OR THING).

----

02 - ONCE YOU'VE IDENTIFIED YOUR TRIGGERS, CREATE A HIERARCHY OF EXPOSURE TASKS, START WITH THE TASK OF LEAST ANXIETY AND EXPOSE YOURSELF TO THE TRIGGER FOR A SET AMOUNT OF TIME WITHOUT ENGAGING IN ANY MENTAL COMPULSIVE BEHAVIORS. THIS WILL BE DIFFICULT. TRY TO RESIST PERFORMING ANY COMPULSIVE BEHAVIORS AS THIS WILL ONLY REINFORCE THE OBSESSION.

Triggers Checklist ✔

- ANGRY ☐
- ANNOYED ☐
- ANXIOUS ☐
- ASHAMED ☐
- AWKWARD ☐
- BRAVE ☐
- CALM ☐
- CHEERFUL ☐
- CHILL ☐
- CONFUSED ☐
- DISCOURAGED ☐
- DISTRACTED ☐
- EMBARRASSED ☐
- EXCITED ☐
- FRIENDLY ☐
- GUILTY ☐
- HAPPY ☐
- HOPEFUL ☐
- LONELY ☐
- LOVED ☐
- NERVOUS ☐
- OFFENDED ☐
- SCARED ☐
- THOUGHTFUL ☐
- TIRED ☐
- UNCOMFORTABLE ☐
- UNSURE ☐

PURE OCD
ERP WORKSHEET

03- CONTINUE EXPOSING YOURSELF TO THE TRIGGER UNTIL YOUR ANXIETY LEVEL DECREASES. IT IS IMPORTANT TO MAINTAIN EXPOSURE FOR A SUFFICIENT PERIOD OF TIME AS YOUR BRAIN WILL BECOME ACCUSTOMED TO THE ANXIETY AND WILL NATURALLY DECREASE.

04- ONCE YOU HAVE BECOME ACCUSTOMED TO THE PREVIOUS EXPOSURE TASK, MOVE ON TO THE NEXT TASK THAT YOU HAVE IDENTIFIED IN THE HIERARCHY, GRADUALLY WORKING ON THE TASK OF MOST CONCERN AND CONTINUING EXPOSURE TO IT AT THE SAME LEVEL FOR HABITUATION.

Daily Mood Checker ✔

NOTE

ERP therapy can be difficult and may take time to show results. But the most important thing is to train regularly and constantly to make progress....

OVERCOMING PURE O.C.D THROUGH D.B.T

IN THIS TABLE, TRY TO UNDERSTAND THE OUTBURSTS OF INTRUSIVE THOUGHTS THAT YOU EXPERIENCE FROM TIME TO TIME.
(AT WORK, MEETINGS...ETC)
DISCUSS THEIR IMPACT ON ASPECTS OF YOUR LIFE, AND WHAT COPING SKILLS DO YOU THINK WORK WHEN YOU USE THEM? CONSISTENTLY RATE HOW SUCCESSFUL YOU ARE IN APPLYING THESE SKILLS?

• DISTRESS • INTERPERSONAL EFFECTIVENESS • EMOTIONAL REGULATION PROBLEMS	COPING SKILLS OR PREVENTION IDEAS OR SKILLS
	👍
	✋

DAILY MOOD CYCLE

Instructions: Think about your day from start to finish. Color the first square to express your feelings each time of the day. Next, write a word that reflects your feelings, and draw in the circle a picture of your face that reflects your feelings at that moment.

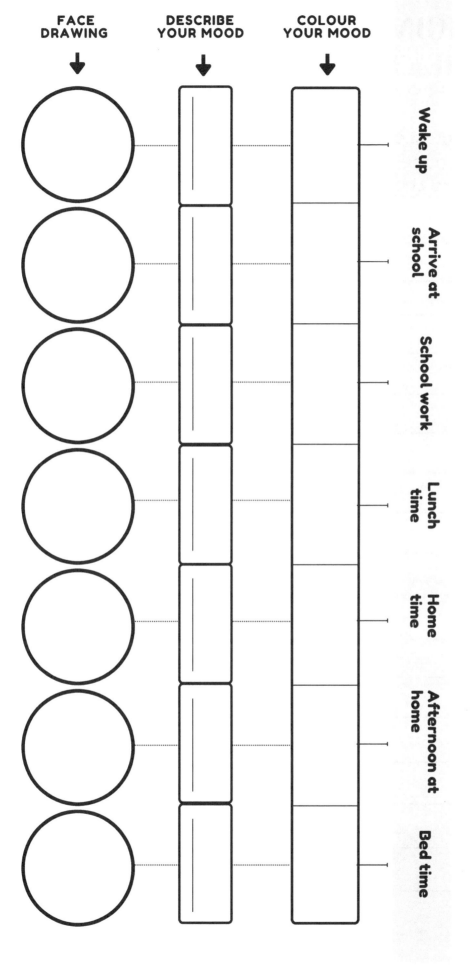

FACE DRAWING

DESCRIBE YOUR MOOD

COLOUR YOUR MOOD

Wake up

Arrive at school

School work

Lunch time

Home time

Afternoon at home

Bed time

CHALLENGING PURE O - DBT WORKSHEET

Date :................................

This section is dedicated to recording all the events of your daily experience with pure obsessive-compulsive disorder and the effects of intrusive thoughts on your quality of life.

_____

_____

_____

_____

_____

_____

_____

_____

_____

_____

_____

_____

_____

_____

_____

_____

PURE OCD SYMPTOMS

PURE "O" SYMPTOMS	SEVERITY	MON	TUES	WED	THUR	FRI	SAT	SUN

PURE O
CBT WORKSHEET

Write down your thoughts, feelings, and behaviors related to your Pure O symptoms. Record the date, time, and any triggers that led to your symptoms.

⊘ —:—

⊘ —:—

⊘ —:—

⊘ —:—

⊘ —:—

⊘ —:—

Daily Mood Checker ✓

ANGRY	☐
ANNOYED	☐
ANXIOUS	☐
ASHAMED	☐
AWKWARD	☐
BRAVE	☐
CALM	☐
CHEERFUL	☐
CHILL	☐
CONFUSED	☐
DISCOURAGED	☐
DISTRACTED	☐
EMBARRASSED	☐
EXCITED	☐
FRIENDLY	☐
GUILTY	☐
HAPPY	☐
HOPEFUL	☐
LONELY	☐
LOVED	☐
NERVOUS	☐
OFFENDED	☐
SCARED	☐
THOUGHTFUL	☐
TIRED	☐
UNCOMFORTABLE	☐
UNSURE	☐

PURE OCD
ERP WORKSHEET

01 - IDENTIFY TRIGGERS: IDENTIFY THE SPECIFIC TRIGGERS THAT CAUSE YOUR INTRUSIVE THOUGHTS.
(A CERTAIN IDEA OR FEELING)
(A SPECIFIC SITUATION OR THING).

02 - ONCE YOU'VE IDENTIFIED YOUR TRIGGERS, CREATE A HIERARCHY OF EXPOSURE TASKS, START WITH THE TASK OF LEAST ANXIETY AND EXPOSE YOURSELF TO THE TRIGGER FOR A SET AMOUNT OF TIME WITHOUT ENGAGING IN ANY MENTAL COMPULSIVE BEHAVIORS. THIS WILL BE DIFFICULT. TRY TO RESIST PERFORMING ANY COMPULSIVE BEHAVIORS AS THIS WILL ONLY REINFORCE THE OBSESSION.

Triggers Checklist ✓

- [ ] ANGRY
- [ ] ANNOYED
- [ ] ANXIOUS
- [ ] ASHAMED
- [ ] AWKWARD
- [ ] BRAVE
- [ ] CALM
- [ ] CHEERFUL
- [ ] CHILL
- [ ] CONFUSED
- [ ] DISCOURAGED
- [ ] DISTRACTED
- [ ] EMBARRASSED
- [ ] EXCITED
- [ ] FRIENDLY
- [ ] GUILTY
- [ ] HAPPY
- [ ] HOPEFUL
- [ ] LONELY
- [ ] LOVED
- [ ] NERVOUS
- [ ] OFFENDED
- [ ] SCARED
- [ ] THOUGHTFUL
- [ ] TIRED
- [ ] UNCOMFORTABLE
- [ ] UNSURE

PURE OCD
ERP WORKSHEET

03- CONTINUE EXPOSING YOURSELF TO THE TRIGGER UNTIL YOUR ANXIETY LEVEL DECREASES. IT IS IMPORTANT TO MAINTAIN EXPOSURE FOR A SUFFICIENT PERIOD OF TIME AS YOUR BRAIN WILL BECOME ACCUSTOMED TO THE ANXIETY AND WILL NATURALLY DECREASE.

04- ONCE YOU HAVE BECOME ACCUSTOMED TO THE PREVIOUS EXPOSURE TASK, MOVE ON TO THE NEXT TASK THAT YOU HAVE IDENTIFIED IN THE HIERARCHY, GRADUALLY WORKING ON THE TASK OF MOST CONCERN AND CONTINUING EXPOSURE TO IT AT THE SAME LEVEL FOR HABITUATION.

Daily Mood Checker

NOTE

ERP therapy can be difficult and may take time to show results. But the most important thing is to train regularly and constantly to make progress....

OVERCOMING PURE O.C.D THROUGH D.B.T

IN THIS TABLE, TRY TO UNDERSTAND THE OUTBURSTS OF INTRUSIVE THOUGHTS THAT YOU EXPERIENCE FROM TIME TO TIME.
(AT WORK, MEETINGS...ETC)
DISCUSS THEIR IMPACT ON ASPECTS OF YOUR LIFE, AND WHAT COPING SKILLS DO YOU THINK WORK WHEN YOU USE THEM? CONSISTENTLY RATE HOW SUCCESSFUL YOU ARE IN APPLYING THESE SKILLS?

• DISTRESS • INTERPERSONAL EFFECTIVENESS • EMOTIONAL REGULATION PROBLEMS	COPING SKILLS OR PREVENTION IDEAS OR SKILLS

DAILY MOOD CYCLE

Instructions: Think about your day from start to finish. Color the first square to express your feelings each time of the day. Next, write a word that reflects your feelings, and draw in the circle a picture of your face that reflects your feelings at that moment.

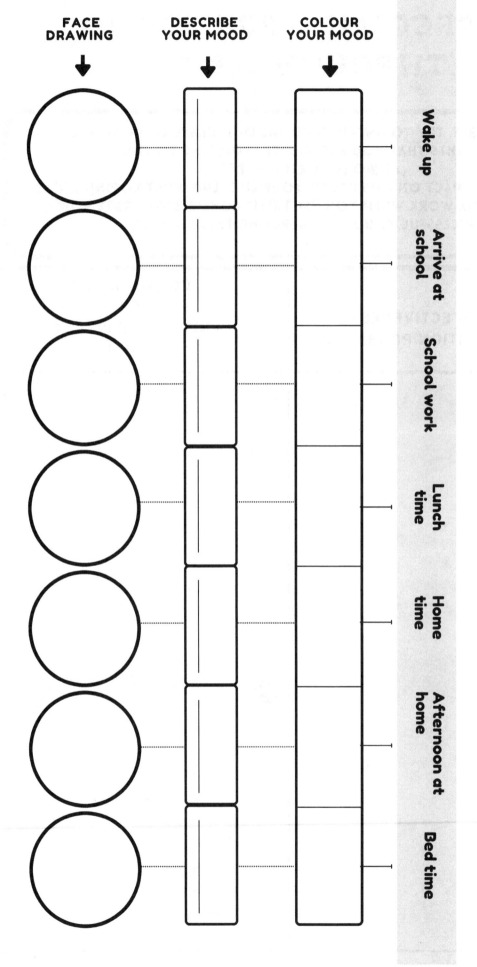

FACE DRAWING

DESCRIBE YOUR MOOD

COLOUR YOUR MOOD

- Wake up
- Arrive at school
- School work
- Lunch time
- Home time
- Afternoon at home
- Bed time

CHALLENGING PURE O - DBT WORKSHEET

A NEW DAY AND AN EFFECTIVE PLAN WORKSHEET

Date :..

This section is dedicated to recording all the events of your daily experience with pure obsessive-compulsive disorder and the effects of intrusive thoughts on your quality of life.

_____

_____

_____

_____

_____

_____

_____

_____

_____

_____

_____

_____

_____

_____

PURE OCD SYMPTOMS

PURE "O" SYMPTOMS	SEVERITY	MON	TUES	WED	THUR	FRI	SAT	SUN

PURE O
CBT WORKSHEET

Write down your thoughts, feelings, and behaviors related to your Pure O symptoms. Record the date, time, and any triggers that led to your symptoms.

⊘ —— : ——

⊘ —— : ——

⊘ —— : ——

⊘ —— : ——

⊘ —— : ——

⊘ —— : ——

Daily Mood Checker ✔

ANGRY	☐
ANNOYED	☐
ANXIOUS	☐
ASHAMED	☐
AWKWARD	☐
BRAVE	☐
CALM	☐
CHEERFUL	☐
CHILL	☐
CONFUSED	☐
DISCOURAGED	☐
DISTRACTED	☐
EMBARRASSED	☐
EXCITED	☐
FRIENDLY	☐
GUILTY	☐
HAPPY	☐
HOPEFUL	☐
LONELY	☐
LOVED	☐
NERVOUS	☐
OFFENDED	☐
SCARED	☐
THOUGHTFUL	☐
TIRED	☐
UNCOMFORTABLE	☐
UNSURE	☐

PURE OCD
ERP WORKSHEET

01 - IDENTIFY TRIGGERS: IDENTIFY THE SPECIFIC
TRIGGERS THAT CAUSE YOUR INTRUSIVE THOUGHTS.
(A CERTAIN IDEA OR FEELING)
(A SPECIFIC SITUATION OR THING).

----

02 - ONCE YOU'VE IDENTIFIED YOUR TRIGGERS, CREATE A
HIERARCHY OF EXPOSURE TASKS, START WITH THE TASK
OF LEAST ANXIETY AND EXPOSE YOURSELF TO THE
TRIGGER FOR A SET AMOUNT OF TIME WITHOUT
ENGAGING IN ANY MENTAL COMPULSIVE BEHAVIORS. THIS
WILL BE DIFFICULT. TRY TO RESIST PERFORMING ANY
COMPULSIVE BEHAVIORS AS THIS WILL ONLY REINFORCE
THE OBSESSION.

Triggers Checklist ✔

- ANGRY ☐
- ANNOYED ☐
- ANXIOUS ☐
- ASHAMED ☐
- AWKWARD ☐
- BRAVE ☐
- CALM ☐
- CHEERFUL ☐
- CHILL ☐
- CONFUSED ☐
- DISCOURAGED ☐
- DISTRACTED ☐
- EMBARRASSED ☐
- EXCITED ☐
- FRIENDLY ☐
- GUILTY ☐
- HAPPY ☐
- HOPEFUL ☐
- LONELY ☐
- LOVED ☐
- NERVOUS ☐
- OFFENDED ☐
- SCARED ☐
- THOUGHTFUL ☐
- TIRED ☐
- UNCOMFORTABLE ☐
- UNSURE ☐

PURE OCD
ERP WORKSHEET

03- CONTINUE EXPOSING YOURSELF TO THE TRIGGER UNTIL YOUR ANXIETY LEVEL DECREASES. IT IS IMPORTANT TO MAINTAIN EXPOSURE FOR A SUFFICIENT PERIOD OF TIME AS YOUR BRAIN WILL BECOME ACCUSTOMED TO THE ANXIETY AND WILL NATURALLY DECREASE.

04- ONCE YOU HAVE BECOME ACCUSTOMED TO THE PREVIOUS EXPOSURE TASK, MOVE ON TO THE NEXT TASK THAT YOU HAVE IDENTIFIED IN THE HIERARCHY, GRADUALLY WORKING ON THE TASK OF MOST CONCERN AND CONTINUING EXPOSURE TO IT AT THE SAME LEVEL FOR HABITUATION.

Daily Mood Checker

NOTE

ERP therapy can be difficult and may take time to show results. But the most important thing is to train regularly and constantly to make progress....

OVERCOMING PURE O.C.D THROUGH D.B.T

IN THIS TABLE, TRY TO UNDERSTAND THE OUTBURSTS OF INTRUSIVE THOUGHTS THAT YOU EXPERIENCE FROM TIME TO TIME.
(AT WORK, MEETINGS...ETC)
DISCUSS THEIR IMPACT ON ASPECTS OF YOUR LIFE, AND WHAT COPING SKILLS DO YOU THINK WORK WHEN YOU USE THEM? CONSISTENTLY RATE HOW SUCCESSFUL YOU ARE IN APPLYING THESE SKILLS?

• DISTRESS • INTERPERSONAL EFFECTIVENESS • EMOTIONAL REGULATION PROBLEMS	COPING SKILLS OR PREVENTION IDEAS OR SKILLS

DAILY MOOD CYCLE

Instructions: Think about your day from start to finish. Color the first square to express your feelings each time of the day. Next, write a word that reflects your feelings, and draw in the circle a picture of your face that reflects your feelings at that moment.

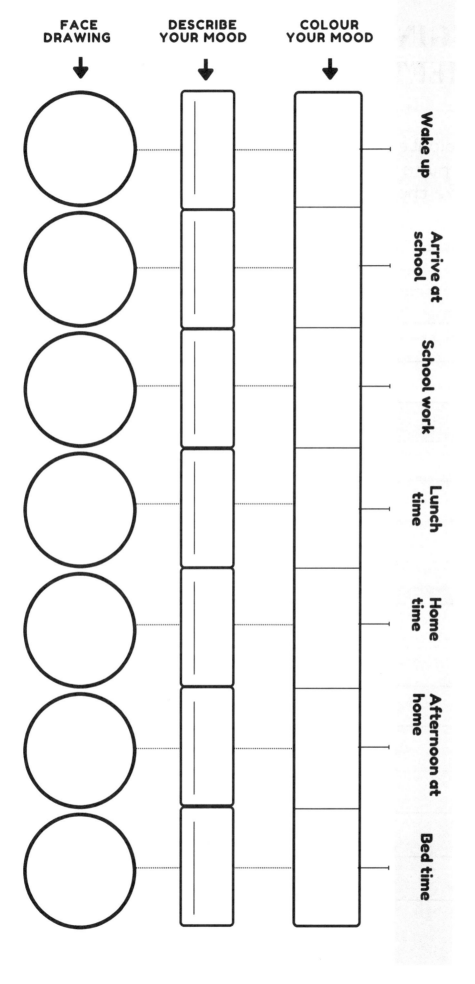

FACE DRAWING

DESCRIBE YOUR MOOD

COLOUR YOUR MOOD

Wake up

Arrive at school

School work

Lunch time

Home time

Afternoon at home

Bed time

CHALLENGING PURE O - DBT WORKSHEET

A NEW DAY AND AN EFFECTIVE PLAN WORKSHEET

Date :..

This section is dedicated to recording all the events of your daily experience with pure obsessive-compulsive disorder and the effects of intrusive thoughts on your quality of life.

_____

_____

_____

_____

_____

_____

_____

_____

_____

_____

_____

_____

_____

_____

_____

_____

PURE OCD SYMPTOMS

PURE "O" SYMPTOMS	SEVERITY	MON	TUES	WED	THUR	FRI	SAT	SUN

PURE O
CBT WORKSHEET

Write down your thoughts, feelings, and behaviors related to your Pure O symptoms. Record the date, time, and any triggers that led to your symptoms.

Daily Mood Checker ✓

Mood	
ANGRY	☐
ANNOYED	☐
ANXIOUS	☐
ASHAMED	☐
AWKWARD	☐
BRAVE	☐
CALM	☐
CHEERFUL	☐
CHILL	☐
CONFUSED	☐
DISCOURAGED	☐
DISTRACTED	☐
EMBARRASSED	☐
EXCITED	☐
FRIENDLY	☐
GUILTY	☐
HAPPY	☐
HOPEFUL	☐
LONELY	☐
LOVED	☐
NERVOUS	☐
OFFENDED	☐
SCARED	☐
THOUGHTFUL	☐
TIRED	☐
UNCOMFORTABLE	☐
UNSURE	☐

PURE OCD
ERP WORKSHEET

01 - IDENTIFY TRIGGERS: IDENTIFY THE SPECIFIC
TRIGGERS THAT CAUSE YOUR INTRUSIVE THOUGHTS.
(A CERTAIN IDEA OR FEELING)
(A SPECIFIC SITUATION OR THING).

02 - ONCE YOU'VE IDENTIFIED YOUR TRIGGERS, CREATE A
HIERARCHY OF EXPOSURE TASKS, START WITH THE TASK
OF LEAST ANXIETY AND EXPOSE YOURSELF TO THE
TRIGGER FOR A SET AMOUNT OF TIME WITHOUT
ENGAGING IN ANY MENTAL COMPULSIVE BEHAVIORS. THIS
WILL BE DIFFICULT. TRY TO RESIST PERFORMING ANY
COMPULSIVE BEHAVIORS AS THIS WILL ONLY REINFORCE
THE OBSESSION.

Triggers Checklist

- ANGRY ☐
- ANNOYED ☐
- ANXIOUS ☐
- ASHAMED ☐
- AWKWARD ☐
- BRAVE ☐
- CALM ☐
- CHEERFUL ☐
- CHILL ☐
- CONFUSED ☐
- DISCOURAGED ☐
- DISTRACTED ☐
- EMBARRASSED ☐
- EXCITED ☐
- FRIENDLY ☐
- GUILTY ☐
- HAPPY ☐
- HOPEFUL ☐
- LONELY ☐
- LOVED ☐
- NERVOUS ☐
- OFFENDED ☐
- SCARED ☐
- THOUGHTFUL ☐
- TIRED ☐
- UNCOMFORTABLE ☐
- UNSURE ☐

Date :

Sleep quality :

Daily Mood Checker ✓

03- CONTINUE EXPOSING YOURSELF TO THE TRIGGER UNTIL YOUR ANXIETY LEVEL DECREASES. IT IS IMPORTANT TO MAINTAIN EXPOSURE FOR A SUFFICIENT PERIOD OF TIME AS YOUR BRAIN WILL BECOME ACCUSTOMED TO THE ANXIETY AND WILL NATURALLY DECREASE.

04- ONCE YOU HAVE BECOME ACCUSTOMED TO THE PREVIOUS EXPOSURE TASK, MOVE ON TO THE NEXT TASK THAT YOU HAVE IDENTIFIED IN THE HIERARCHY, GRADUALLY WORKING ON THE TASK OF MOST CONCERN AND CONTINUING EXPOSURE TO IT AT THE SAME LEVEL FOR HABITUATION.

NOTE

ERP therapy can be difficult and may take time to show results. But the most important thing is to train regularly and constantly to make progress....

OVERCOMING PURE O.C.D THROUGH D.B.T

IN THIS TABLE, TRY TO UNDERSTAND THE OUTBURSTS OF INTRUSIVE
THOUGHTS THAT YOU EXPERIENCE FROM TIME TO TIME.
(AT WORK, MEETINGS...ETC)
DISCUSS THEIR IMPACT ON ASPECTS OF YOUR LIFE, AND WHAT COPING SKILLS
DO YOU THINK WORK WHEN YOU USE THEM? CONSISTENTLY RATE HOW
SUCCESSFUL YOU ARE IN APPLYING THESE SKILLS?

• DISTRESS • INTERPERSONAL EFFECTIVENESS • EMOTIONAL REGULATION PROBLEMS	COPING SKILLS OR PREVENTION IDEAS OR SKILLS

DAILY MOOD CYCLE

Instructions: Think about your day from start to finish. Color the first square to express your feelings each time of the day. Next, write a word that reflects your feelings, and draw in the circle a picture of your face that reflects your feelings at that moment.

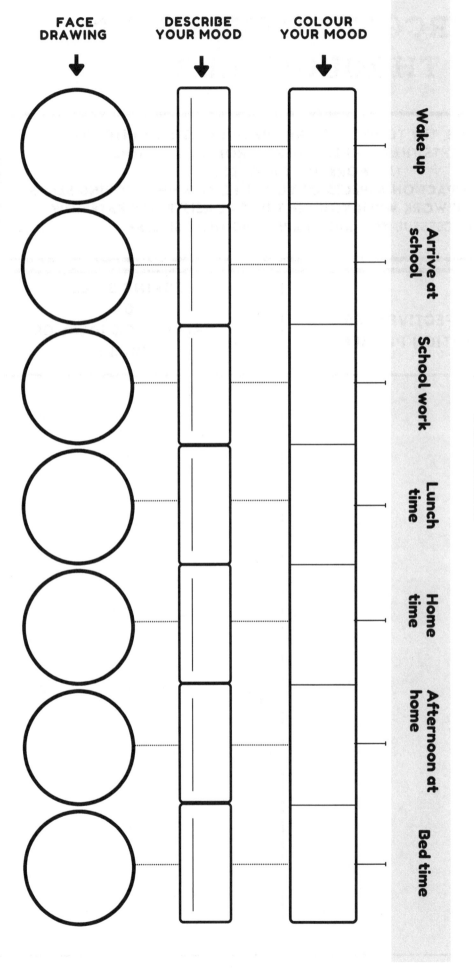

FACE DRAWING

DESCRIBE YOUR MOOD

COLOUR YOUR MOOD

Wake up

Arrive at school

School work

Lunch time

Home time

Afternoon at home

Bed time

CHALLENGING PURE O - DBT WORKSHEET

Date :.................................

This section is dedicated to recording all the events of your daily experience with pure obsessive-compulsive disorder and the effects of intrusive thoughts on your quality of life.

_____

_____

_____

_____

_____

_____

_____

_____

_____

_____

_____

_____

_____

_____

_____

_____

_____

PURE OCD SYMPTOMS

PURE "O" SYMPTOMS	SEVERITY	MON	TUES	WED	THUR	FRI	SAT	SUN

PURE O
CBT WORKSHEET

Write down your thoughts, feelings, and behaviors related to your Pure O symptoms. Record the date, time, and any triggers that led to your symptoms.

○ __ : __

○ __ : __

○ __ : __

○ __ : __

○ __ : __

○ __ : __

Daily Mood Checker ✓

ANGRY	☐
ANNOYED	☐
ANXIOUS	☐
ASHAMED	☐
AWKWARD	☐
BRAVE	☐
CALM	☐
CHEERFUL	☐
CHILL	☐
CONFUSED	☐
DISCOURAGED	☐
DISTRACTED	☐
EMBARRASSED	☐
EXCITED	☐
FRIENDLY	☐
GUILTY	☐
HAPPY	☐
HOPEFUL	☐
LONELY	☐
LOVED	☐
NERVOUS	☐
OFFENDED	☐
SCARED	☐
THOUGHTFUL	☐
TIRED	☐
UNCOMFORTABLE	☐
UNSURE	☐

PURE OCD
ERP WORKSHEET

01 - IDENTIFY TRIGGERS: IDENTIFY THE SPECIFIC TRIGGERS THAT CAUSE YOUR INTRUSIVE THOUGHTS.
(A CERTAIN IDEA OR FEELING)
(A SPECIFIC SITUATION OR THING).

---

02 - ONCE YOU'VE IDENTIFIED YOUR TRIGGERS, CREATE A HIERARCHY OF EXPOSURE TASKS, START WITH THE TASK OF LEAST ANXIETY AND EXPOSE YOURSELF TO THE TRIGGER FOR A SET AMOUNT OF TIME WITHOUT ENGAGING IN ANY MENTAL COMPULSIVE BEHAVIORS. THIS WILL BE DIFFICULT. TRY TO RESIST PERFORMING ANY COMPULSIVE BEHAVIORS AS THIS WILL ONLY REINFORCE THE OBSESSION.

Triggers Checklist

- [ ] ANGRY
- [ ] ANNOYED
- [ ] ANXIOUS
- [ ] ASHAMED
- [ ] AWKWARD
- [ ] BRAVE
- [ ] CALM
- [ ] CHEERFUL
- [ ] CHILL
- [ ] CONFUSED
- [ ] DISCOURAGED
- [ ] DISTRACTED
- [ ] EMBARRASSED
- [ ] EXCITED
- [ ] FRIENDLY
- [ ] GUILTY
- [ ] HAPPY
- [ ] HOPEFUL
- [ ] LONELY
- [ ] LOVED
- [ ] NERVOUS
- [ ] OFFENDED
- [ ] SCARED
- [ ] THOUGHTFUL
- [ ] TIRED
- [ ] UNCOMFORTABLE
- [ ] UNSURE

PURE OCD
ERP WORKSHEET

Date :

Sleep quality :

03- CONTINUE EXPOSING YOURSELF TO THE TRIGGER UNTIL YOUR ANXIETY LEVEL DECREASES. IT IS IMPORTANT TO MAINTAIN EXPOSURE FOR A SUFFICIENT PERIOD OF TIME AS YOUR BRAIN WILL BECOME ACCUSTOMED TO THE ANXIETY AND WILL NATURALLY DECREASE.

Daily Mood Checker ✓

04- ONCE YOU HAVE BECOME ACCUSTOMED TO THE PREVIOUS EXPOSURE TASK, MOVE ON TO THE NEXT TASK THAT YOU HAVE IDENTIFIED IN THE HIERARCHY, GRADUALLY WORKING ON THE TASK OF MOST CONCERN AND CONTINUING EXPOSURE TO IT AT THE SAME LEVEL FOR HABITUATION.

NOTE

ERP therapy can be difficult and may take time to show results. But the most important thing is to train regularly and constantly to make progress....

OVERCOMING PURE O.C.D THROUGH D.B.T

IN THIS TABLE, TRY TO UNDERSTAND THE OUTBURSTS OF INTRUSIVE
THOUGHTS THAT YOU EXPERIENCE FROM TIME TO TIME.
(AT WORK, MEETINGS...ETC)
DISCUSS THEIR IMPACT ON ASPECTS OF YOUR LIFE, AND WHAT COPING SKILLS
DO YOU THINK WORK WHEN YOU USE THEM? CONSISTENTLY RATE HOW
SUCCESSFUL YOU ARE IN APPLYING THESE SKILLS?

DISTRESS • INTERPERSONAL EFFECTIVENESS • EMOTIONAL REGULATION PROBLEMS	COPING SKILLS OR PREVENTION IDEAS OR SKILLS

DAILY MOOD CYCLE

Instructions: Think about your day from start to finish. Color the first square to express your feelings each time of the day. Next, write a word that reflects your feelings, and draw in the circle a picture of your face that reflects your feelings at that moment.

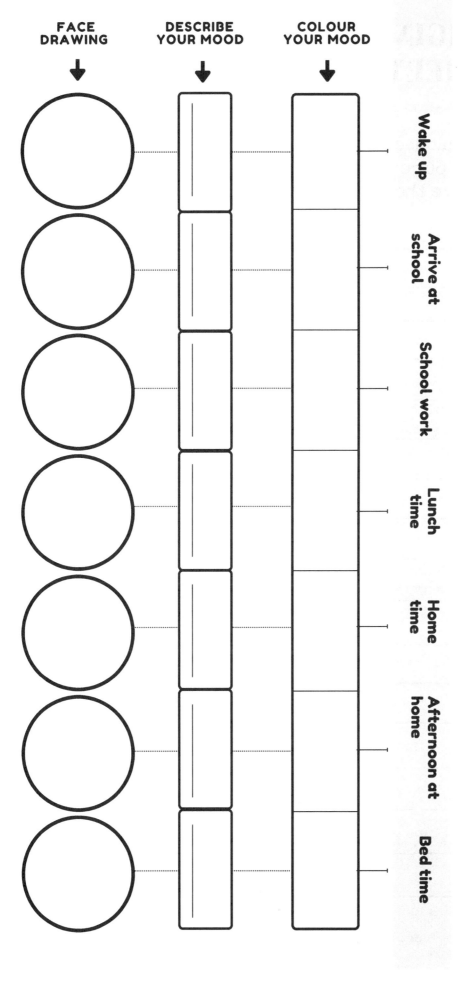

FACE DRAWING

DESCRIBE YOUR MOOD

COLOUR YOUR MOOD

Wake up

Arrive at school

School work

Lunch time

Home time

Afternoon at home

Bed time

CHALLENGING PURE O - DBT WORKSHEET

Date :................................

This section is dedicated to recording all the events of your daily experience with pure obsessive-compulsive disorder and the effects of intrusive thoughts on your quality of life.

_____

_____

_____

_____

_____

_____

_____

_____

_____

_____

_____

_____

_____

_____

_____

PURE OCD SYMPTOMS

PURE "O" SYMPTOMS	SEVERITY	MON	TUES	WED	THUR	FRI	SAT	SUN

PURE O
CBT WORKSHEET

Write down your thoughts, feelings, and behaviors related to your Pure O symptoms. Record the date, time, and any triggers that led to your symptoms.

⊘ —— : ——

⊘ —— : ——

⊘ —— : ——

⊘ —— : ——

⊘ —— : ——

⊘ —— : ——

Daily Mood Checker ✓

ANGRY	☐
ANNOYED	☐
ANXIOUS	☐
ASHAMED	☐
AWKWARD	☐
BRAVE	☐
CALM	☐
CHEERFUL	☐
CHILL	☐
CONFUSED	☐
DISCOURAGED	☐
DISTRACTED	☐
EMBARRASSED	☐
EXCITED	☐
FRIENDLY	☐
GUILTY	☐
HAPPY	☐
HOPEFUL	☐
LONELY	☐
LOVED	☐
NERVOUS	☐
OFFENDED	☐
SCARED	☐
THOUGHTFUL	☐
TIRED	☐
UNCOMFORTABLE	☐
UNSURE	☐

PURE OCD
ERP WORKSHEET

01 - IDENTIFY TRIGGERS: IDENTIFY THE SPECIFIC TRIGGERS THAT CAUSE YOUR INTRUSIVE THOUGHTS.
(A CERTAIN IDEA OR FEELING)
(A SPECIFIC SITUATION OR THING).

02 - ONCE YOU'VE IDENTIFIED YOUR TRIGGERS, CREATE A HIERARCHY OF EXPOSURE TASKS, START WITH THE TASK OF LEAST ANXIETY AND EXPOSE YOURSELF TO THE TRIGGER FOR A SET AMOUNT OF TIME WITHOUT ENGAGING IN ANY MENTAL COMPULSIVE BEHAVIORS. THIS WILL BE DIFFICULT. TRY TO RESIST PERFORMING ANY COMPULSIVE BEHAVIORS AS THIS WILL ONLY REINFORCE THE OBSESSION.

Triggers Checklist

- [ ] ANGRY
- [ ] ANNOYED
- [ ] ANXIOUS
- [ ] ASHAMED
- [ ] AWKWARD
- [ ] BRAVE
- [ ] CALM
- [ ] CHEERFUL
- [ ] CHILL
- [ ] CONFUSED
- [ ] DISCOURAGED
- [ ] DISTRACTED
- [ ] EMBARRASSED
- [ ] EXCITED
- [ ] FRIENDLY
- [ ] GUILTY
- [ ] HAPPY
- [ ] HOPEFUL
- [ ] LONELY
- [ ] LOVED
- [ ] NERVOUS
- [ ] OFFENDED
- [ ] SCARED
- [ ] THOUGHTFUL
- [ ] TIRED
- [ ] UNCOMFORTABLE
- [ ] UNSURE

03- CONTINUE EXPOSING YOURSELF TO THE TRIGGER UNTIL YOUR ANXIETY LEVEL DECREASES. IT IS IMPORTANT TO MAINTAIN EXPOSURE FOR A SUFFICIENT PERIOD OF TIME AS YOUR BRAIN WILL BECOME ACCUSTOMED TO THE ANXIETY AND WILL NATURALLY DECREASE.

04- ONCE YOU HAVE BECOME ACCUSTOMED TO THE PREVIOUS EXPOSURE TASK, MOVE ON TO THE NEXT TASK THAT YOU HAVE IDENTIFIED IN THE HIERARCHY, GRADUALLY WORKING ON THE TASK OF MOST CONCERN AND CONTINUING EXPOSURE TO IT AT THE SAME LEVEL FOR HABITUATION.

NOTE

ERP therapy can be difficult and may take time to show results. But the most important thing is to train regularly and constantly to make progress....

OVERCOMING PURE O.C.D
THROUGH D.B.T

IN THIS TABLE, TRY TO UNDERSTAND THE OUTBURSTS OF INTRUSIVE
THOUGHTS THAT YOU EXPERIENCE FROM TIME TO TIME.
(AT WORK, MEETINGS...ETC)
DISCUSS THEIR IMPACT ON ASPECTS OF YOUR LIFE, AND WHAT COPING SKILLS
DO YOU THINK WORK WHEN YOU USE THEM? CONSISTENTLY RATE HOW
SUCCESSFUL YOU ARE IN APPLYING THESE SKILLS?

• DISTRESS • INTERPERSONAL EFFECTIVENESS • EMOTIONAL REGULATION PROBLEMS	COPING SKILLS OR PREVENTION IDEAS OR SKILLS

DAILY MOOD CYCLE

Instructions: Think about your day from start to finish. Color the first square to express your feelings each time of the day. Next, write a word that reflects your feelings, and draw in the circle a picture of your face that reflects your feelings at that moment.

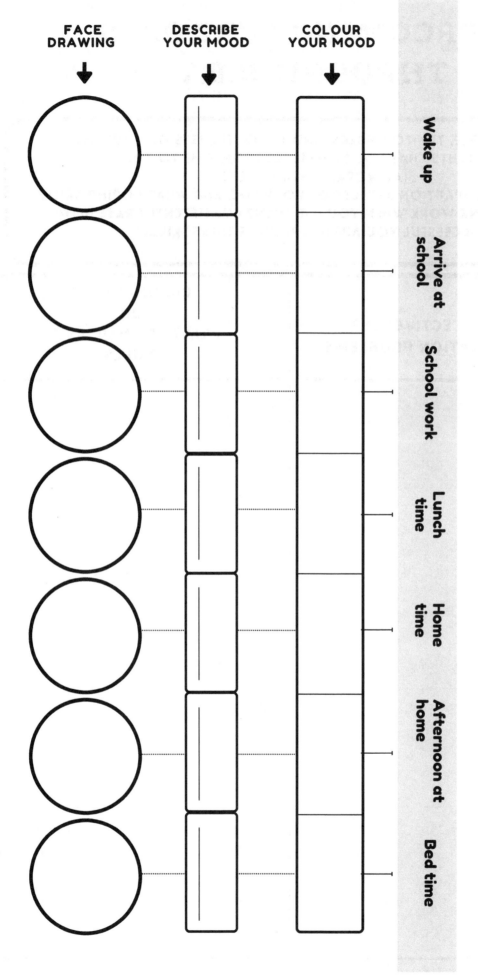

FACE DRAWING

DESCRIBE YOUR MOOD

COLOUR YOUR MOOD

- Wake up
- Arrive at school
- School work
- Lunch time
- Home time
- Afternoon at home
- Bed time

CHALLENGING PURE O - DBT WORKSHEET

A NEW DAY AND AN EFFECTIVE PLAN WORKSHEET

Date :................................

This section is dedicated to recording all the events of your daily experience with pure obsessive-compulsive disorder and the effects of intrusive thoughts on your quality of life.

_____

_____

_____

_____

_____

_____

_____

_____

_____

_____

_____

_____

_____

_____

PURE OCD SYMPTOMS

PURE "O" SYMPTOMS	SEVERITY	MON	TUES	WED	THUR	FRI	SAT	SUN

PURE O
CBT WORKSHEET

Write down your thoughts, feelings, and behaviors related to your Pure O symptoms. Record the date, time, and any triggers that led to your symptoms.

⊘ —— : ——

⊘ —— : ——

⊘ —— : ——

⊘ —— : ——

⊘ —— : ——

⊘ —— : ——

Daily Mood Checker ✓

ANGRY	☐
ANNOYED	☐
ANXIOUS	☐
ASHAMED	☐
AWKWARD	☐
BRAVE	☐
CALM	☐
CHEERFUL	☐
CHILL	☐
CONFUSED	☐
DISCOURAGED	☐
DISTRACTED	☐
EMBARRASSED	☐
EXCITED	☐
FRIENDLY	☐
GUILTY	☐
HAPPY	☐
HOPEFUL	☐
LONELY	☐
LOVED	☐
NERVOUS	☐
OFFENDED	☐
SCARED	☐
THOUGHTFUL	☐
TIRED	☐
UNCOMFORTABLE	☐
UNSURE	☐

PURE OCD
ERP WORKSHEET

Date :

Sleep quality :

01 - IDENTIFY TRIGGERS: IDENTIFY THE SPECIFIC TRIGGERS THAT CAUSE YOUR INTRUSIVE THOUGHTS.
(A CERTAIN IDEA OR FEELING)
(A SPECIFIC SITUATION OR THING).

---

02 - ONCE YOU'VE IDENTIFIED YOUR TRIGGERS, CREATE A HIERARCHY OF EXPOSURE TASKS, START WITH THE TASK OF LEAST ANXIETY AND EXPOSE YOURSELF TO THE TRIGGER FOR A SET AMOUNT OF TIME WITHOUT ENGAGING IN ANY MENTAL COMPULSIVE BEHAVIORS. THIS WILL BE DIFFICULT. TRY TO RESIST PERFORMING ANY COMPULSIVE BEHAVIORS AS THIS WILL ONLY REINFORCE THE OBSESSION.

Triggers Checklist ✔

- ANGRY ☐
- ANNOYED ☐
- ANXIOUS ☐
- ASHAMED ☐
- AWKWARD ☐
- BRAVE ☐
- CALM ☐
- CHEERFUL ☐
- CHILL ☐
- CONFUSED ☐
- DISCOURAGED ☐
- DISTRACTED ☐
- EMBARRASSED ☐
- EXCITED ☐
- FRIENDLY ☐
- GUILTY ☐
- HAPPY ☐
- HOPEFUL ☐
- LONELY ☐
- LOVED ☐
- NERVOUS ☐
- OFFENDED ☐
- SCARED ☐
- THOUGHTFUL ☐
- TIRED ☐
- UNCOMFORTABLE ☐
- UNSURE ☐

PURE OCD
ERP WORKSHEET

03- CONTINUE EXPOSING YOURSELF TO THE TRIGGER UNTIL YOUR ANXIETY LEVEL DECREASES. IT IS IMPORTANT TO MAINTAIN EXPOSURE FOR A SUFFICIENT PERIOD OF TIME AS YOUR BRAIN WILL BECOME ACCUSTOMED TO THE ANXIETY AND WILL NATURALLY DECREASE.

Daily Mood Checker ✔

☐
☐
☐
☐
☐
☐
☐
☐
☐
☐
☐

04- ONCE YOU HAVE BECOME ACCUSTOMED TO THE PREVIOUS EXPOSURE TASK, MOVE ON TO THE NEXT TASK THAT YOU HAVE IDENTIFIED IN THE HIERARCHY, GRADUALLY WORKING ON THE TASK OF MOST CONCERN AND CONTINUING EXPOSURE TO IT AT THE SAME LEVEL FOR HABITUATION.

☐
☐
☐
☐
☐
☐
☐
☐
☐
☐
☐
☐
☐
☐
☐

NOTE

ERP therapy can be difficult and may take time to show results. But the most important thing is to train regularly and constantly to make progress....

OVERCOMING PURE O.C.D THROUGH D.B.T

IN THIS TABLE, TRY TO UNDERSTAND THE OUTBURSTS OF INTRUSIVE THOUGHTS THAT YOU EXPERIENCE FROM TIME TO TIME.
(AT WORK, MEETINGS...ETC)
DISCUSS THEIR IMPACT ON ASPECTS OF YOUR LIFE, AND WHAT COPING SKILLS DO YOU THINK WORK WHEN YOU USE THEM? CONSISTENTLY RATE HOW SUCCESSFUL YOU ARE IN APPLYING THESE SKILLS?

• DISTRESS • INTERPERSONAL EFFECTIVENESS • EMOTIONAL REGULATION PROBLEMS	COPING SKILLS OR PREVENTION IDEAS OR SKILLS

DAILY MOOD CYCLE

Instructions: Think about your day from start to finish. Color the first square to express your feelings each time of the day. Next, write a word that reflects your feelings, and draw in the circle a picture of your face that reflects your feelings at that moment.

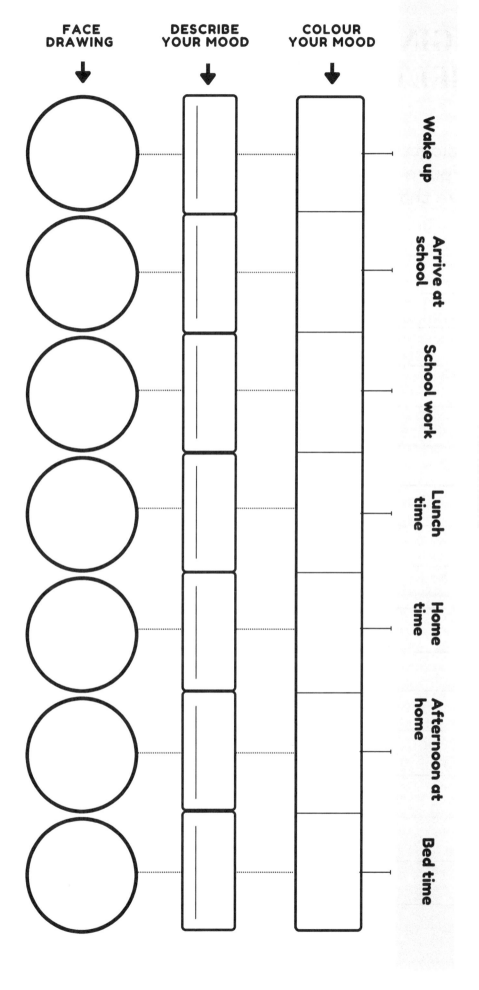

FACE DRAWING

DESCRIBE YOUR MOOD

COLOUR YOUR MOOD

Wake up

Arrive at school

School work

Lunch time

Home time

Afternoon at home

Bed time

CHALLENGING PURE O - DBT WORKSHEET

Date :..

This section is dedicated to recording all the events of your daily experience with pure obsessive-compulsive disorder and the effects of intrusive thoughts on your quality of life.

_____

_____

_____

_____

_____

_____

_____

_____

_____

_____

_____

_____

_____

_____

PURE OCD SYMPTOMS

PURE "O" SYMPTOMS	SEVERITY	MON	TUES	WED	THUR	FRI	SAT	SUN

PURE O
CBT WORKSHEET

Write down your thoughts, feelings, and behaviors related to your Pure O symptoms. Record the date, time, and any triggers that led to your symptoms.

⊘ —:—

⊘ —:—

⊘ —:—

⊘ —:—

⊘ —:—

⊘ —:—

Daily Mood Checker ✓

ANGRY	☐
ANNOYED	☐
ANXIOUS	☐
ASHAMED	☐
AWKWARD	☐
BRAVE	☐
CALM	☐
CHEERFUL	☐
CHILL	☐
CONFUSED	☐
DISCOURAGED	☐
DISTRACTED	☐
EMBARRASSED	☐
EXCITED	☐
FRIENDLY	☐
GUILTY	☐
HAPPY	☐
HOPEFUL	☐
LONELY	☐
LOVED	☐
NERVOUS	☐
OFFENDED	☐
SCARED	☐
THOUGHTFUL	☐
TIRED	☐
UNCOMFORTABLE	☐
UNSURE	☐

PURE OCD
ERP WORKSHEET

01 - IDENTIFY TRIGGERS: IDENTIFY THE SPECIFIC TRIGGERS THAT CAUSE YOUR INTRUSIVE THOUGHTS.
(A CERTAIN IDEA OR FEELING)
(A SPECIFIC SITUATION OR THING).

02 - ONCE YOU'VE IDENTIFIED YOUR TRIGGERS, CREATE A HIERARCHY OF EXPOSURE TASKS, START WITH THE TASK OF LEAST ANXIETY AND EXPOSE YOURSELF TO THE TRIGGER FOR A SET AMOUNT OF TIME WITHOUT ENGAGING IN ANY MENTAL COMPULSIVE BEHAVIORS. THIS WILL BE DIFFICULT. TRY TO RESIST PERFORMING ANY COMPULSIVE BEHAVIORS AS THIS WILL ONLY REINFORCE THE OBSESSION.

Triggers Checklist

- ANGRY ☐
- ANNOYED ☐
- ANXIOUS ☐
- ASHAMED ☐
- AWKWARD ☐
- BRAVE ☐
- CALM ☐
- CHEERFUL ☐
- CHILL ☐
- CONFUSED ☐
- DISCOURAGED ☐
- DISTRACTED ☐
- EMBARRASSED ☐
- EXCITED ☐
- FRIENDLY ☐
- GUILTY ☐
- HAPPY ☐
- HOPEFUL ☐
- LONELY ☐
- LOVED ☐
- NERVOUS ☐
- OFFENDED ☐
- SCARED ☐
- THOUGHTFUL ☐
- TIRED ☐
- UNCOMFORTABLE ☐
- UNSURE ☐

Date :

Sleep quality :

Daily Mood Checker

03- CONTINUE EXPOSING YOURSELF TO THE TRIGGER UNTIL YOUR ANXIETY LEVEL DECREASES. IT IS IMPORTANT TO MAINTAIN EXPOSURE FOR A SUFFICIENT PERIOD OF TIME AS YOUR BRAIN WILL BECOME ACCUSTOMED TO THE ANXIETY AND WILL NATURALLY DECREASE.

04- ONCE YOU HAVE BECOME ACCUSTOMED TO THE PREVIOUS EXPOSURE TASK, MOVE ON TO THE NEXT TASK THAT YOU HAVE IDENTIFIED IN THE HIERARCHY, GRADUALLY WORKING ON THE TASK OF MOST CONCERN AND CONTINUING EXPOSURE TO IT AT THE SAME LEVEL FOR HABITUATION.

NOTE

ERP therapy can be difficult and may take time to show results. But the most important thing is to train regularly and constantly to make progress....

OVERCOMING PURE O.C.D THROUGH D.B.T

IN THIS TABLE, TRY TO UNDERSTAND THE OUTBURSTS OF INTRUSIVE THOUGHTS THAT YOU EXPERIENCE FROM TIME TO TIME.
(AT WORK, MEETINGS...ETC)
DISCUSS THEIR IMPACT ON ASPECTS OF YOUR LIFE, AND WHAT COPING SKILLS DO YOU THINK WORK WHEN YOU USE THEM? CONSISTENTLY RATE HOW SUCCESSFUL YOU ARE IN APPLYING THESE SKILLS?

• DISTRESS • INTERPERSONAL EFFECTIVENESS • EMOTIONAL REGULATION PROBLEMS	COPING SKILLS OR PREVENTION IDEAS OR SKILLS

DAILY MOOD CYCLE

Instructions: Think about your day from start to finish. Color the first square to express your feelings each time of the day. Next, write a word that reflects your feelings, and draw in the circle a picture of your face that reflects your feelings at that moment.

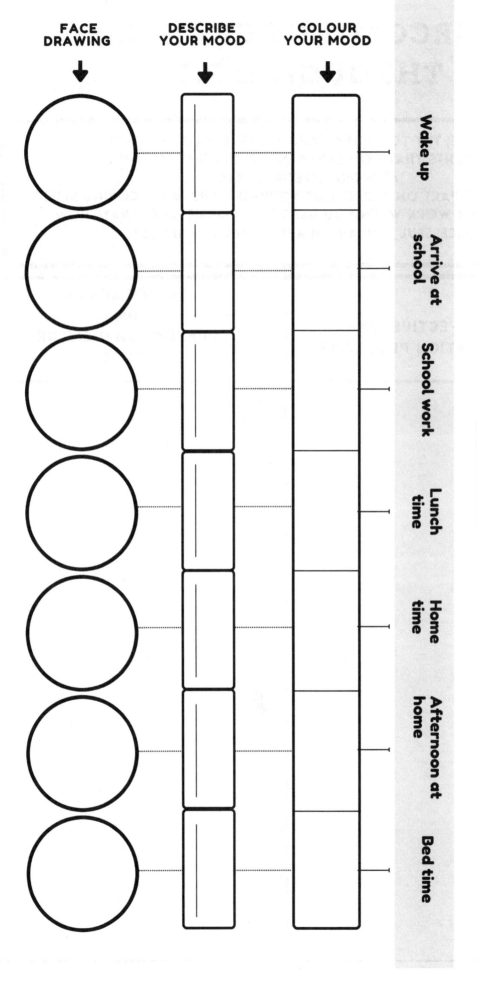

FACE DRAWING

DESCRIBE YOUR MOOD

COLOUR YOUR MOOD

Wake up

Arrive at school

School work

Lunch time

Home time

Afternoon at home

Bed time

CHALLENGING PURE O - DBT WORKSHEET

Date :..

This section is dedicated to recording all the events of your daily experience with pure obsessive-compulsive disorder and the effects of intrusive thoughts on your quality of life.

_____

_____

_____

_____

_____

_____

_____

_____

_____

_____

_____

_____

_____

_____

_____

_____

_____

PURE OCD SYMPTOMS

PURE "O" SYMPTOMS	SEVERITY	MON	TUES	WED	THUR	FRI	SAT	SUN

PURE O
CBT WORKSHEET

Write down your thoughts, feelings, and behaviors related to your Pure O symptoms. Record the date, time, and any triggers that led to your symptoms.

⊘ __ _ __

⊘ __ _ __

⊘ __ _ __

⊘ __ _ __

⊘ __ _ __

⊘ __ _ __

Daily Mood Checker ✓

ANGRY	☐
ANNOYED	☐
ANXIOUS	☐
ASHAMED	☐
AWKWARD	☐
BRAVE	☐
CALM	☐
CHEERFUL	☐
CHILL	☐
CONFUSED	☐
DISCOURAGED	☐
DISTRACTED	☐
EMBARRASSED	☐
EXCITED	☐
FRIENDLY	☐
GUILTY	☐
HAPPY	☐
HOPEFUL	☐
LONELY	☐
LOVED	☐
NERVOUS	☐
OFFENDED	☐
SCARED	☐
THOUGHTFUL	☐
TIRED	☐
UNCOMFORTABLE	☐
UNSURE	☐

PURE OCD
ERP WORKSHEET

01 - IDENTIFY TRIGGERS: IDENTIFY THE SPECIFIC TRIGGERS THAT CAUSE YOUR INTRUSIVE THOUGHTS. (A CERTAIN IDEA OR FEELING) (A SPECIFIC SITUATION OR THING).

---

02 - ONCE YOU'VE IDENTIFIED YOUR TRIGGERS, CREATE A HIERARCHY OF EXPOSURE TASKS, START WITH THE TASK OF LEAST ANXIETY AND EXPOSE YOURSELF TO THE TRIGGER FOR A SET AMOUNT OF TIME WITHOUT ENGAGING IN ANY MENTAL COMPULSIVE BEHAVIORS. THIS WILL BE DIFFICULT. TRY TO RESIST PERFORMING ANY COMPULSIVE BEHAVIORS AS THIS WILL ONLY REINFORCE THE OBSESSION.

Triggers Checklist ✔

- ANGRY ☐
- ANNOYED ☐
- ANXIOUS ☐
- ASHAMED ☐
- AWKWARD ☐
- BRAVE ☐
- CALM ☐
- CHEERFUL ☐
- CHILL ☐
- CONFUSED ☐
- DISCOURAGED ☐
- DISTRACTED ☐
- EMBARRASSED ☐
- EXCITED ☐
- FRIENDLY ☐
- GUILTY ☐
- HAPPY ☐
- HOPEFUL ☐
- LONELY ☐
- LOVED ☐
- NERVOUS ☐
- OFFENDED ☐
- SCARED ☐
- THOUGHTFUL ☐
- TIRED ☐
- UNCOMFORTABLE ☐
- UNSURE ☐

PURE OCD
ERP WORKSHEET

03- CONTINUE EXPOSING YOURSELF TO THE TRIGGER UNTIL YOUR ANXIETY LEVEL DECREASES. IT IS IMPORTANT TO MAINTAIN EXPOSURE FOR A SUFFICIENT PERIOD OF TIME AS YOUR BRAIN WILL BECOME ACCUSTOMED TO THE ANXIETY AND WILL NATURALLY DECREASE.

04- ONCE YOU HAVE BECOME ACCUSTOMED TO THE PREVIOUS EXPOSURE TASK, MOVE ON TO THE NEXT TASK THAT YOU HAVE IDENTIFIED IN THE HIERARCHY, GRADUALLY WORKING ON THE TASK OF MOST CONCERN AND CONTINUING EXPOSURE TO IT AT THE SAME LEVEL FOR HABITUATION.

Daily Mood Checker ✔

☐
☐
☐
☐
☐
☐
☐
☐
☐
☐
☐
☐
☐
☐
☐
☐
☐
☐
☐
☐
☐
☐
☐
☐
☐
☐

NOTE

ERP therapy can be difficult and may take time to show results. But the most important thing is to train regularly and constantly to make progress....

OVERCOMING PURE O.C.D THROUGH D.B.T

IN THIS TABLE, TRY TO UNDERSTAND THE OUTBURSTS OF INTRUSIVE THOUGHTS THAT YOU EXPERIENCE FROM TIME TO TIME.
(AT WORK, MEETINGS...ETC)
DISCUSS THEIR IMPACT ON ASPECTS OF YOUR LIFE, AND WHAT COPING SKILLS DO YOU THINK WORK WHEN YOU USE THEM? CONSISTENTLY RATE HOW SUCCESSFUL YOU ARE IN APPLYING THESE SKILLS?

• DISTRESS • INTERPERSONAL EFFECTIVENESS • EMOTIONAL REGULATION PROBLEMS	COPING SKILLS OR PREVENTION IDEAS OR SKILLS

DAILY MOOD CYCLE

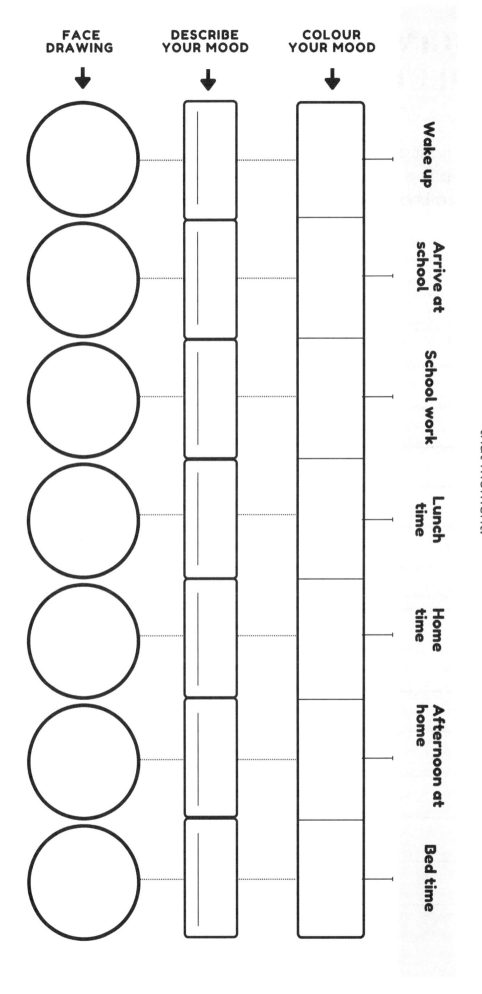

FACE DRAWING

DESCRIBE YOUR MOOD

COLOUR YOUR MOOD

Wake up

Arrive at school

School work

Lunch time

Home time

Afternoon at home

Bed time

CHALLENGING PURE O - DBT WORKSHEET

A NEW DAY AND AN EFFECTIVE PLAN WORKSHEET

Date :...............................

This section is dedicated to recording all the events of your daily experience with pure obsessive-compulsive disorder and the effects of intrusive thoughts on your quality of life.

_____

_____

_____

_____

_____

_____

_____

_____

_____

_____

_____

_____

_____

PURE OCD SYMPTOMS

PURE "O" SYMPTOMS	SEVERITY	MON	TUES	WED	THUR	FRI	SAT	SUN

PURE O
CBT WORKSHEET

Write down your thoughts, feelings, and behaviors related to your Pure O symptoms. Record the date, time, and any triggers that led to your symptoms.

⊘ —:— _____

_____

_____

_____

⊘ —:— _____

_____

_____

_____

⊘ —:— _____

_____

_____

_____

⊘ —:— _____

_____

_____

_____

⊘ —:— _____

_____

_____

_____

⊘ —:— _____

_____

_____

Daily Mood Checker ✓

Mood	
ANGRY	☐
ANNOYED	☐
ANXIOUS	☐
ASHAMED	☐
AWKWARD	☐
BRAVE	☐
CALM	☐
CHEERFUL	☐
CHILL	☐
CONFUSED	☐
DISCOURAGED	☐
DISTRACTED	☐
EMBARRASSED	☐
EXCITED	☐
FRIENDLY	☐
GUILTY	☐
HAPPY	☐
HOPEFUL	☐
LONELY	☐
LOVED	☐
NERVOUS	☐
OFFENDED	☐
SCARED	☐
THOUGHTFUL	☐
TIRED	☐
UNCOMFORTABLE	☐
UNSURE	☐

PURE OCD
ERP WORKSHEET

01 - IDENTIFY TRIGGERS: IDENTIFY THE SPECIFIC TRIGGERS THAT CAUSE YOUR INTRUSIVE THOUGHTS.
(A CERTAIN IDEA OR FEELING)
(A SPECIFIC SITUATION OR THING).

02 - ONCE YOU'VE IDENTIFIED YOUR TRIGGERS, CREATE A HIERARCHY OF EXPOSURE TASKS, START WITH THE TASK OF LEAST ANXIETY AND EXPOSE YOURSELF TO THE TRIGGER FOR A SET AMOUNT OF TIME WITHOUT ENGAGING IN ANY MENTAL COMPULSIVE BEHAVIORS. THIS WILL BE DIFFICULT. TRY TO RESIST PERFORMING ANY COMPULSIVE BEHAVIORS AS THIS WILL ONLY REINFORCE THE OBSESSION.

Triggers Checklist

- ANGRY ☐
- ANNOYED ☐
- ANXIOUS ☐
- ASHAMED ☐
- AWKWARD ☐
- BRAVE ☐
- CALM ☐
- CHEERFUL ☐
- CHILL ☐
- CONFUSED ☐
- DISCOURAGED ☐
- DISTRACTED ☐
- EMBARRASSED ☐
- EXCITED ☐
- FRIENDLY ☐
- GUILTY ☐
- HAPPY ☐
- HOPEFUL ☐
- LONELY ☐
- LOVED ☐
- NERVOUS ☐
- OFFENDED ☐
- SCARED ☐
- THOUGHTFUL ☐
- TIRED ☐
- UNCOMFORTABLE ☐
- UNSURE ☐

PURE OCD
ERP WORKSHEET

03- CONTINUE EXPOSING YOURSELF TO THE TRIGGER UNTIL YOUR ANXIETY LEVEL DECREASES. IT IS IMPORTANT TO MAINTAIN EXPOSURE FOR A SUFFICIENT PERIOD OF TIME AS YOUR BRAIN WILL BECOME ACCUSTOMED TO THE ANXIETY AND WILL NATURALLY DECREASE.

Daily Mood Checker ✔

04- ONCE YOU HAVE BECOME ACCUSTOMED TO THE PREVIOUS EXPOSURE TASK, MOVE ON TO THE NEXT TASK THAT YOU HAVE IDENTIFIED IN THE HIERARCHY, GRADUALLY WORKING ON THE TASK OF MOST CONCERN AND CONTINUING EXPOSURE TO IT AT THE SAME LEVEL FOR HABITUATION.

NOTE

ERP therapy can be difficult and may take time to show results. But the most important thing is to train regularly and constantly to make progress....

OVERCOMING PURE O.C.D THROUGH D.B.T

IN THIS TABLE, TRY TO UNDERSTAND THE OUTBURSTS OF INTRUSIVE THOUGHTS THAT YOU EXPERIENCE FROM TIME TO TIME.
(AT WORK, MEETINGS...ETC)
DISCUSS THEIR IMPACT ON ASPECTS OF YOUR LIFE, AND WHAT COPING SKILLS DO YOU THINK WORK WHEN YOU USE THEM? CONSISTENTLY RATE HOW SUCCESSFUL YOU ARE IN APPLYING THESE SKILLS?

• DISTRESS • INTERPERSONAL EFFECTIVENESS • EMOTIONAL REGULATION PROBLEMS	COPING SKILLS OR PREVENTION IDEAS OR SKILLS

DAILY MOOD CYCLE

Instructions: Think about your day from start to finish. Color the first square to express your feelings each time of the day. Next, write a word that reflects your feelings, and draw in the circle a picture of your face that reflects your feelings at that moment.

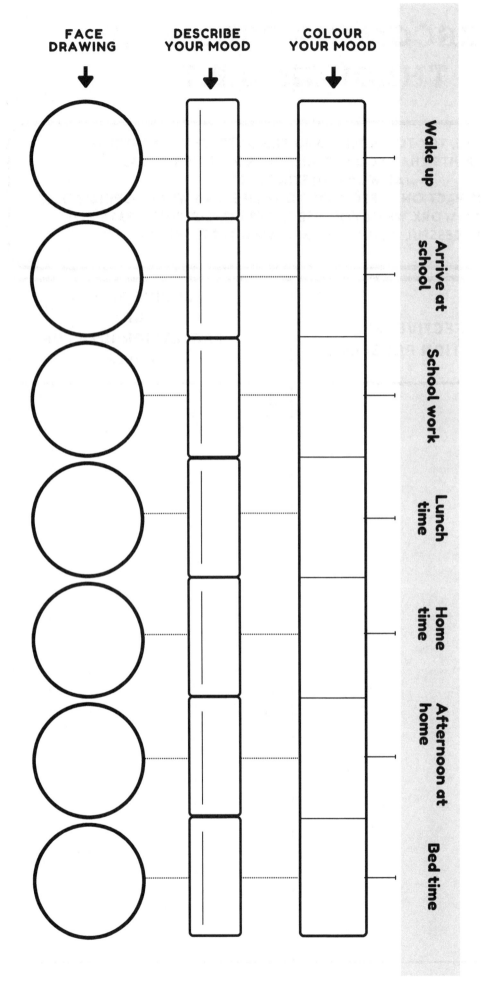

FACE DRAWING

DESCRIBE YOUR MOOD

COLOUR YOUR MOOD

Wake up

Arrive at school

School work

Lunch time

Home time

Afternoon at home

Bed time

CHALLENGING PURE O - DBT WORKSHEET

Date : ....

This section is dedicated to recording all the events of your daily experience with pure obsessive-compulsive disorder and the effects of intrusive thoughts on your quality of life.

_____

_____

_____

_____

_____

_____

_____

_____

_____

_____

_____

_____

_____

PURE OCD SYMPTOMS

PURE "O" SYMPTOMS	SEVERITY	MON	TUES	WED	THUR	FRI	SAT	SUN

PURE O
CBT WORKSHEET

Write down your thoughts, feelings, and behaviors related to your Pure O symptoms. Record the date, time, and any triggers that led to your symptoms.

⊘ —— : ——

⊘ —— : ——

⊘ —— : ——

⊘ —— : ——

⊘ —— : ——

⊘ —— : ——

Daily Mood Checker ✓

ANGRY	☐
ANNOYED	☐
ANXIOUS	☐
ASHAMED	☐
AWKWARD	☐
BRAVE	☐
CALM	☐
CHEERFUL	☐
CHILL	☐
CONFUSED	☐
DISCOURAGED	☐
DISTRACTED	☐
EMBARRASSED	☐
EXCITED	☐
FRIENDLY	☐
GUILTY	☐
HAPPY	☐
HOPEFUL	☐
LONELY	☐
LOVED	☐
NERVOUS	☐
OFFENDED	☐
SCARED	☐
THOUGHTFUL	☐
TIRED	☐
UNCOMFORTABLE	☐
UNSURE	☐

PURE OCD
ERP WORKSHEET

Date :

Sleep quality :

01 - IDENTIFY TRIGGERS: IDENTIFY THE SPECIFIC TRIGGERS THAT CAUSE YOUR INTRUSIVE THOUGHTS.
(A CERTAIN IDEA OR FEELING)
(A SPECIFIC SITUATION OR THING).

----

02 - ONCE YOU'VE IDENTIFIED YOUR TRIGGERS, CREATE A HIERARCHY OF EXPOSURE TASKS, START WITH THE TASK OF LEAST ANXIETY AND EXPOSE YOURSELF TO THE TRIGGER FOR A SET AMOUNT OF TIME WITHOUT ENGAGING IN ANY MENTAL COMPULSIVE BEHAVIORS. THIS WILL BE DIFFICULT. TRY TO RESIST PERFORMING ANY COMPULSIVE BEHAVIORS AS THIS WILL ONLY REINFORCE THE OBSESSION.

Triggers Checklist ✓

- ANGRY ☐
- ANNOYED ☐
- ANXIOUS ☐
- ASHAMED ☐
- AWKWARD ☐
- BRAVE ☐
- CALM ☐
- CHEERFUL ☐
- CHILL ☐
- CONFUSED ☐
- DISCOURAGED ☐
- DISTRACTED ☐
- EMBARRASSED ☐
- EXCITED ☐
- FRIENDLY ☐
- GUILTY ☐
- HAPPY ☐
- HOPEFUL ☐
- LONELY ☐
- LOVED ☐
- NERVOUS ☐
- OFFENDED ☐
- SCARED ☐
- THOUGHTFUL ☐
- TIRED ☐
- UNCOMFORTABLE ☐
- UNSURE ☐

PURE OCD
ERP WORKSHEET

03- CONTINUE EXPOSING YOURSELF TO THE TRIGGER UNTIL YOUR ANXIETY LEVEL DECREASES. IT IS IMPORTANT TO MAINTAIN EXPOSURE FOR A SUFFICIENT PERIOD OF TIME AS YOUR BRAIN WILL BECOME ACCUSTOMED TO THE ANXIETY AND WILL NATURALLY DECREASE.

Daily Mood Checker ✓

04- ONCE YOU HAVE BECOME ACCUSTOMED TO THE PREVIOUS EXPOSURE TASK, MOVE ON TO THE NEXT TASK THAT YOU HAVE IDENTIFIED IN THE HIERARCHY, GRADUALLY WORKING ON THE TASK OF MOST CONCERN AND CONTINUING EXPOSURE TO IT AT THE SAME LEVEL FOR HABITUATION.

NOTE

ERP therapy can be difficult and may take time to show results. But the most important thing is to train regularly and constantly to make progress....

OVERCOMING PURE O.C.D THROUGH D.B.T

IN THIS TABLE, TRY TO UNDERSTAND THE OUTBURSTS OF INTRUSIVE THOUGHTS THAT YOU EXPERIENCE FROM TIME TO TIME.
(AT WORK, MEETINGS...ETC)
DISCUSS THEIR IMPACT ON ASPECTS OF YOUR LIFE, AND WHAT COPING SKILLS DO YOU THINK WORK WHEN YOU USE THEM? CONSISTENTLY RATE HOW SUCCESSFUL YOU ARE IN APPLYING THESE SKILLS?

• DISTRESS • INTERPERSONAL EFFECTIVENESS • EMOTIONAL REGULATION PROBLEMS	COPING SKILLS OR PREVENTION IDEAS OR SKILLS

DAILY MOOD CYCLE

Instructions: Think about your day from start to finish. Color the first square to express your feelings each time of the day. Next, write a word that reflects your feelings, and draw in the circle a picture of your face that reflects your feelings at that moment.

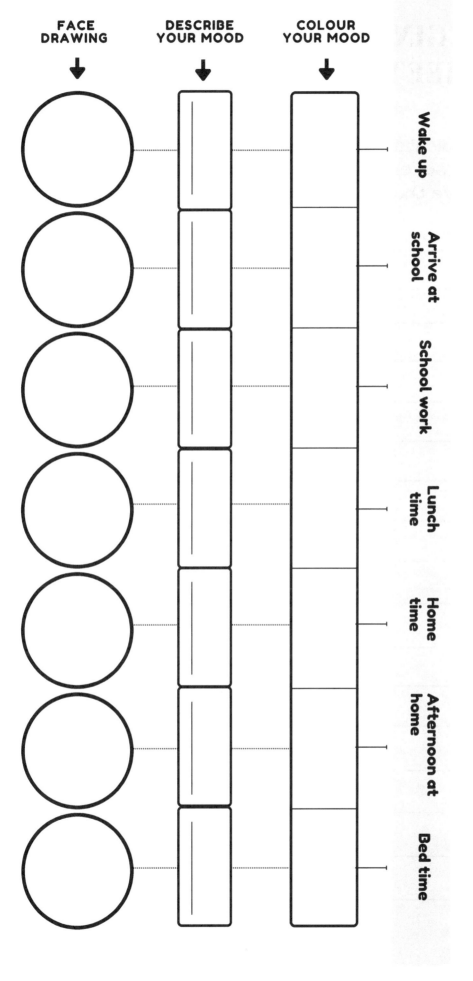

FACE DRAWING

DESCRIBE YOUR MOOD

COLOUR YOUR MOOD

Wake up

Arrive at school

School work

Lunch time

Home time

Afternoon at home

Bed time

CHALLENGING PURE O - DBT WORKSHEET

Date :.................................

This section is dedicated to recording all the events of your daily experience with pure obsessive-compulsive disorder and the effects of intrusive thoughts on your quality of life.

_____

_____

_____

_____

_____

_____

_____

_____

_____

_____

_____

_____

_____

_____

Made in United States
Troutdale, OR
05/30/2024

20216022R10058